STOCKHOLM SYNDROME

or

Remember That Time Jimmy's All American Beefsteak Restaurant Was Taken Over By That Group of Radicals?

An immersive play with music

Adam Szymkowicz

BROADWAY PLAY PUBLISHING INC
New York
www.broadwayplaypub.com
info@broadwayplaypub.com

Cover photo by John B Barrois

First edition: October 2022
I S B N: 978-0-88145-955-5

Book design: Marie Donovan
Page make-up: Adobe InDesign
Typeface: Palatino

For A.J. Allegra

STOCKHOLM SYNDROME was commissioned by and premiered at The NOLA Project, New Orleans, at the Little Gem Saloon. It opened 16 January 2019. The cast and creative contributors were:

BRIAN.. Keith Claverie
MEL.. Kathleen Moore
JANE .... Julie Dietz
ANGIE .... April Louise
RED .... Bill Mader
SUE JEAN........................ Rebecca Elizabeth Hollingsworth
MARTY.. Michael Krikorian
LYNX .... Kristin Shoffner
RAZOR.. Alec Barnes
MARTYNA ....Leslie Claverie
JIMMY...Mark Routhier
WILLIAM .... Michael Pepp
LILY MAE...Nadia Eiler

Director .... A.J. Allegra
Music .... Jack Craft & Skyler Stroup
Assistant Director... James Yeargain
Musical Director.. Ainsley Matich
Choreographer..Kali Russell
Production Manager..................................... Megan Harms
Stage Manager ....Sarah Chatelain
Assistant Stage Manager.................................... Tova Steele
Scenic/Prop Designer.. Ellen Bull
Costume Designer... Erin Routh
Lighting Designer ....Jasmine Williams
Sound Designer ....Betsy Primes
Production photography .... Edward Carter Simon

Special Thanks in no particular order to A.J. and the incredible cast and crew at The NOLA Project, Jack and Skyler, James Bartelle, Todd D'Amour.

John and Rhoda Szymkowicz, Seth Glewen, The Gersh Agency, Maggie Toole, Tricia O'Toole, Tish Dace, Kristen Palmer, Wallace Szymkowicz, Elizabeth Bochain. Joe Kraemer.

Kip and Michael and BPPI.

At Juilliard, Tony Meneses, Brian Watkins, Donja Love, Morgan Gould, Matthew Capodicasa, Eboni Booth, Jessica Huang, Margot Connolly, Marsha Norman, David Lindsey-Abaire. Evan Yionoulis, Richard Feldman, Kathy Hood, Jerry Shafnisky, Sarah Wells, Kaitlin Springston, Brittany Giles-Jones, James Gregg, Lindsey Alexander, Gaven Trinidad. Tanya Barfield, Stephen Brown, Daniella De Jesús, Lia Romeo, Nick Kaidoo, Jake Brasch, Yilong Liu, Nia Akilah Robinson, Jordan Ramirez Puckett. Derrick Sanders, Hannah Rubenstein, Aly Homminga, Laila Perlman, Jenny Lord.

Little Gem Saloon, Nick and Maria Bazan, Willow School, Patrick Sean McCrea, Mandi Wood, Alex Smith, Amy and Brian Eiler, Will Addison, Thomas Baumgardner, The Radical Buffoon(s), The Tennessee Williams Theatre Company of New Orleans, Tulane University Department of Theatre and Dance, Hahnville High School.

CHARACTERS

(6M, 6F. Actors can be any race.)

Employees:
BRIAN, *male, the manager, thinly veiled desperation*
MEL, *female, chipper, excited to serve you*
JANE, *female, anti-establishment, not excited to serve you,*
  MEL'*s twin sister (they don't have to look alike)*
ANGIE, *female, been there too long*
RED, *male, the cook, smokes a lot of pot*

Interlopers:
LYNX, *female, the crew's leader*
RAZOR, *male, the silent type, dangerous, large*
MARTYNA, *female, psychotic, Eastern European accent*

Customers:
SUE JEAN, *female*
MARTY, *male*

The Past:
YOUNG JIMMY, *20s, possibly played by the actor playing*
  BRIAN
YOUNG LILY MAE, *6, possibly played by the actress who*
  plays LYNX
Note: The NOLA Project did this as a video, using the actor
playing JIMMY *and a young girl playing* YOUNG LILY MAE.

The Outsider:
WILLIAM, *male, efficient, all business*

The Boss, The Legend:
JIMMY

SETTING

Jimmy's All American Beefsteak Restaurant

The décor is tacky. A big chain restaurant. You know the type. Corporate Office hopes instead of going home to your family you will come to Jimmy's on Fridays after work where you can drink a large scorpion bowl, maybe two and eat their unlimited signature Jumbo Jimbo Onion Rings™. Don't forget to take a photo and #tweetyourmeal. Fun! So much fun! "It's America's place."

Ideally the set is the restaurant and the action happens all around the audience who sit at tables and can order large alcoholic beverages and maybe some food. Immersive, y'all.

Time: Now. Or in the case I accidentally put something in the play that dates it, like whatever year this play is published. But ideally, this is happening right now.

NOTE

I highly recommend that productions use the music and revised lyrics created by Jack Craft and Skyler Stroup which can be procured by e-mailing them at craftandstroup@gmail.com

(The play opens with audience members brought into the theater in small groups and seated by actors playing waitstaff and possibly by waitstaff if there is waitstaff.)

(Here is sample introductory text after seating and handing out menus)

Welcome to Jimmy's All American Beefsteak Restaurant. My name is _____. I'll be your chipper server of chipped beef and other beefly and beeflike delectables. Can I get you started with a beefsteak or a Jimmy's Choice Extreme Size Alcoholic Beverage? Our drink special today is the Jimmy and Gin Personal Bucket. We also have a Lily Mae with Lemon for the kiddies and teetotalers and the designated driver guests we like to call Jimmy's Friends. Be a friend to Jimmy, be safe. Can I get you an Extreme Size bucket or scorpion bowl or a flaming rum barrel or a beefsteak? Is it beef? Is it steak? Yes.

(After everyone is seated, and some people have drinks, The employees—minus RED—***sing** *to* SUE JEAN *and* MARTY, *the audience plants, at their table.*

EMPLOYEES: Happy Happy Birthday Birthday! Happy Birthday Happy Birthday. It's a happy birthday to you. Whoo! From all of us *(ALL OF US)* to all of you *(ALL OF YOU)*! Happy Happy Birthday! Happy Happy Birthday! Happy Happy Birthday! WHOOO!

MEL: Here's a jumbo Jimmy Beefcake from Jimmy's All American to you.

(Someone places a gray piece of meat with a lit candle in front of MARTY. *He blows out the candle and they all leave.)*

SUE JEAN: Oh wow, Marty.

MARTY: Yup.

SUE JEAN: Lookit that!

MARTY: Yup.

SUE JEAN: Looks like real beef.

MARTY: Beefcake, yup.

SUE JEAN: I like the bread here too.

MARTY: Me too. Me too. Yup.

SUE JEAN: Happy birthday, Marty.

MARTY: Thanks, Sue Jean.

(A huddle of employees. RED *comes out for this. He is flagrantly smoking a joint.)*

BRIAN: All right everyone. Quiet down. Just a few small announcements before we get too busy.

JANE: Can we talk about the explosions for a second?

BRIAN: You don't have to worry about that.

ANGIE: We don't?

BRIAN: It's a non-issue.

JANE: But—

MEL: Brian says it's a non-issue.

BRIAN: Good. Good. A few things. *(He looks at his clipboard.)* One: Push the apps and the specials. We're still under quota on Jimmy Con Quesos. Remember to upsize on drink orders. Two: Keep the energy up and out. I want to see Jimmy Smiles the whole time. I mean it, people. We got to be shipshape and Jimmy Fresh. Jimmy himself has been doing visitations again.

JANE: Really?

ANGIE: I hear that, yeah.

BRIAN: And because we are the historical first location of Jimmy's All American, he's bound to visit, maybe even tonight.

JANE: This was the first Jimmy's?

BRIAN: Of course.

MEL: I told you that.

JANE: I don't always listen to you when you talk.

BRIAN: It's really exciting actually.

(BRIAN *points to a children's wagon mounted on the wall. A spotlight on the wagon. Magical music*)

BRIAN: That right there is Lily Mae's actual childhood wagon. You know, from the commercials?

JANE: Oh.

BRIAN: Yes. "Daddy, I'm hungry."

JANE: Sure. "Daddy, I'm hungry."

BRIAN: There's a lot of history. I feel it. Every day here. The gravity of what we're doing. A lot of weight on our shoulders. But we can bear it and thrive even under the weight of it. Because we are an amazing team. Well trained. A finely-tuned machine. And we are chipper, aren't we?

(*All ad lib, yes we are, I guess so, etc.*)

BRIAN: All in for the cheer.

ANGIE: Hey, uh, Brian, before we start—

BRIAN: What's up, Angie?

ANGIE: I'm just wondering—you said—if there was news about—raises.

BRIAN: Oh, yes! Well, I have an email into corporate. I haven't heard yet but I have a good feeling.

ANGIE: It's just that there haven't been any for a couple years now.

BRIAN: Right. Well, that's why I think this year, it's real likely.

ANGIE: Okay. All right. It's just that I could really use that money.

BRIAN: I'll let you know as soon as I know.

JANE: Brian—

BRIAN: Later. All in now.

(They all put their hands in for a cheer.)

ALL: JIMMY! JIMMY! JIMMY!

JANE: So you don't think the place will explode tonight then?

BRIAN: Of course not.

(Song starts)

BRIAN: Nothing bad can ever happen at Jimmy's
    Beefsteak Place
When you're here, you're comfy and you're home
Nothing bad can ever happen at Jimmy's Beefsteak
    Place
When you're here, you'll never be alone.
Two steaks for the price of one steak

MEL: All you can eat filler uppers

RED: And steak.

ANGIE: Onions in all different size and shape

RED: And steak.

JANE: Deep fried potato dippers

RED: And steak.

MEL: Chicken flavored dumplings

RED: And steak.

BRIAN: And the salad bar is all that you can take.

ALL: Steak. steak. steak.

(Spoken)

JANE: And you sure we won't get blown up?

BRIAN: That's just rumors.

JANE: It was on the news. Two Jimmy's franchises been blown up so far.

BRIAN: Don't believe TV news. It's an exaggeration.

JANE: So they weren't blown up?

BRIAN: Well, no one was inside when they caught on fire.

JANE: The last one was only twenty miles away.

BRIAN: Yeah, so we're safe. Like lightning.

JANE: I just want to know if I'm going to die tonight.

BRIAN: P'shaw. No one died yet.

(Song)

BRIAN: Nothing bad can ever happen at Jimmy's
    Beefsteak Place
When you're here, you're comfy and you're home
Nothing bad can ever happen at Jimmy's Beefsteak
    Place
When you're here, you'll never be alone.

RED: The roaches rule the kitchen

ALL: Steak.

MEL: *(To JANE)* Why you always bitchin'?

ALL: Steak.

JANE: They eat all the bread and never tip.

ALL: Steak. Steak. Steak.

ANGIE: My feet my legs my back ache
I can't smell another crab cake

It's getting urgent for me
To have surgery
On my hip

ALL: Steak.

RED: Busboys are always ditchin'.

ALL: Steak.

ANGIE: My toes are always itchin'.

ALL: Steak.

JANE: I can't get through a shift without a nip.

(JANE *takes a swig from her flask. Everyone looks away.*)

ALL: Steak. Steak. Steak.

JANE: But so how do you know this Jimmy's won't get attacked too? Especially if it's the first location? We're especially vulnerable.

BRIAN: It's just not something to worry about.

JANE: But—

BRIAN: No.

EVERYONE: Nothing bad can ever happen at Jimmy's Beefsteak Place
When you're here, you're comfy and you're home
Nothing bad can ever happen at Jimmy's Beefsteak Place
When you're here, you'll never be alone.
Nothing bad can ever happen at Jimmy's Beefsteak Place
When you're here, you're comfy and you're home
Nothing bad can ever happen at Jimmy's Beefsteak Place
When you're here, you'll never be alone.

(BRIAN's *phone makes a very loud beep noise. He looks down.*)

BRIAN: Oh. There will be no raises this year.

(Everyone groans. They scatter to get back to work.)

Scene Two

(A frame like we're watching on TV. YOUNG JIMMY [20s] is pulling YOUNG LILY MAE [6] in the wagon previously mentioned. Maybe we pull it off the wall for this scene.)

YOUNG LILY MAE: Daddy, I'm hungry!

YOUNG JIMMY: Oh Lily Mae! You know daddy loves you, right?

YOUNG LILY MAE: Yes.

YOUNG JIMMY: Well I'm always looking for new ways to show you how much I love you. What if I told you there's a place that feels like home except cozier and the sandwiches are warm and fresh and there's bread and pasta and salad and there's a thing called a beefsteak that's what I imagine heaven is like.

YOUNG LILY MAE: I want to eat it.

YOUNG JIMMY: That's my girl!

(YOUNG JIMMY and YOUNG LILY MAE both smile at the camera.)

(Jingle probably sung live as they hold their smile:)

ALL: Jimmy's All American: The American Food
    America Wants

Scene Three

(The restaurant comes alive again. Everyone is rushing, busy. MEL stops JANE as she tries to pass with a tray or something.)

MEL: Hey!

JANE: Not now, Mel.

MEL: Yes, now. I need to talk to you.

(RED *steps out of the kitchen.*)

RED: *(To* JANE*)* Hey.

JANE: Hey.

RED: I got a minute.

JANE: Cool.

MEL: Aren't we in the middle of the rush, right now?

RED: Yeah. Kind of the start of it. I'll be over there.

(RED *goes.* JANE *watches him go.*)

MEL: You have to do better.

JANE: He's okay.

MEL: I don't mean him. I mean, I do mean him. You can do better. But I mean here at work you have to be better at it. Take it seriously.

JANE: Why?

MEL: I got you this job. You're making me look bad.

JANE: Who cares?

MEL: It reflects badly on me if my sister is doing badly.

JANE: Does it?

MEL: Yes.

JANE: Okay. So what? Why do you care? It's just a job.

MEL: It's not just a job.

JANE: A dumb job.

MEL: This is my life, Jane. And you are not going to mess it up for me.

JANE: I feel like there's something you're not telling me.

MEL: We're not kids anymore. It's time to grow up. Act like an adult.

JANE: Put on my *Jimmy Smile*?

MEL: Yes.

JANE: It's a bullshit job, Mel.

MEL: Then get a job somewhere else if you hate it so much.

JANE: I will.

MEL: But until then—

JANE: Whatever.

MEL: No, not whatever. Try harder.

JANE: Okay.

MEL: I'm serious.

JANE: Okay.

MEL: Do it.

JANE: I said okay.

(MEL exits. JANE goes over to where RED is.)

RED: She's such a bitch.

JANE: Don't say that. That's my sister.

RED: You don't think she's a bitch?

JANE: Of course she's a bitch. But only I can say that. You can't say that.

RED: Sorry.

(JANE and RED start going at it, removing only enough clothing to get it done. Are they in the kitchen seen through a window or half hidden in the waitstaff area where the computers are and the ketchup? The point is we can only half see them and they are having a quickie.)

Scene Four

(Song. Spot on ANGIE*)*

ANGIE: Every day is the same as the last day.
It'll be better.
Maybe a little better.
I wish for something better.
Today.

(Spot on JANE *and* RED, *going at it.)*

JANE: Faster!

RED: I'm going as fast as I can.

JANE: Just finish!

RED: I'm trying. Are you close?

JANE: Just finish.

RED: Ungh. Ungh.

*(*RED *continues to groan over the following.* JANE *also makes some noises.)*

JANE: Whenever I have sex, and this has always been true, not just with you, but whenever I have sex I think about a long hallway. The décor sometimes changes. Sometimes it has a nautical theme, with paintings of ships on the wall. Sometimes it gets smaller and smaller the further down the hallway I go. Sometimes it's bright yellow. Sometimes there are tigers chasing me. Or giant moles. Sometimes it's snowing. Sometimes I'm wading through a flood. Sometimes it's tall green grass. But lately it's been a hallway of door after door after door. Sometimes I knock or try to open them, but none of them budge and I can't find the key. So I go to the next door and the next. And the next. And the next. And the next.

RED: Done!

(Spot on ANGIE*)*

ANGIE: *(Sings)*
Maybe a little better.
A slightly warmer sweater.
To feel a bit unfettered
Today.

(A loud noise. A drill, a jackhammer, stuff like that. Spotlight out. Back on RED *and* JANE.*)*

JANE: What the!

RED: Someone's drilling through the floor!

*(*RED *and* JANE *fix their clothes.* LYNX, RAZOR, MARTYNA *enter, covered in cement dust. Can they come up out of the floor? Or from the kitchen. They have large assault type rifles.* MARTYNA *shoots into the ceiling. The employees enter, maybe duck and cover.)*

LYNX: Attention, everyone! May I have your attention?!
Hi. My name is Lynx and you are all our hostages.
We've thrown chains over the door from the outside.
No one is leaving. Not until we get what we came for.

*(*LYNX *sings.)*

LYNX: We don't want any heroes
Heroes are the first to die
Don't want no robert De Niros
Spidermans falling out of the sky
Don't nobody do nothing
Don't you even try
Consider yourself my hostage
Consider this my sovereign nation
If you consider yourself a hero
You better reconsider your consideration
Because
We don't want any heroes
Heroes are the first to die
Don't wa—

(MARTY's *phone rings. It's really loud and only gets louder and louder. So loud it disrupts the song. He answers it.*)

MARTY: Hello? Maybe. I don't know. It's a pretty good birthday, thanks! Except, well I may be a hostage. I guess I'm not sure exactly what's happening. I don't know. How are the kids? Uh huh. Uh huh. Oh.

LYNX: What are you doing!! No phones!

(LYNX *grabs his phone.* RAZOR *hands her a baseball bat. She beats the phone mercilessly. It is so dead.*)

LYNX: Everyone shut off your fucking phone! Now! (*To* MARTYNA) Get him out of here.

MARTYNA: With pleasure.

(SUE JEAN, *watching her husband taken away:*)

SUE JEAN: Oh, but— Hold on for a second if it's not too much—

LYNX: What?!

SUE JEAN: Nothing.

(MARTYNA *grabs* MARTY *and pulls him into the kitchen or offstage. We hear her hitting him and him yelling, smashing into pots, etc. over the following.*)

BRIAN: Hi. Miss Lynx. Hi.

LYNX: Who are you? You trying to be a hero?

BRIAN: No. I'm the manager here. Let's just pause for a minute and talk about this.

LYNX: What's your name?

BRIAN: Brian.

LYNX: Hi Brian.

BRIAN: Hi. I think if we all just relax for a second, we can get you whatever you want and you can go. Can you lower the guns maybe just for sec.

(LYNX *does nothing.*)

BRIAN: Or put down the bat.

(LYNX *lowers the bat.*)

BRIAN: There, that's better. We have a saying here. About how nothing bad ever happens. And how it's like home here. There's a song. We don't have to go into it right now, but…the point is… We're very hospitable. And we're here to serve the…customer. How can we make you happy?

LYNX: Are you offering me sex?

BRIAN: No. No. No. No. Would that make this go away?

LYNX: No. It'll just make it more interesting.

BRIAN: Oh. Well. I'm flattered of course, but I don't—

LYNX: You don't think so?

BRIAN: It's just. I don't think it would be appropriate. Under the circumstances. In this case, I mean. Whereas—

LYNX: Don't worry. It's not the first time I've been rejected.

BRIAN: No. It's not that. I mean, under different circumstances.

LYNX: If you weren't under duress?

BRIAN: Right. If we had met at church.

LYNX: Church?

BRIAN: Or at a party.

LYNX: What kind of parties do you go to, Brian?

BRIAN: Oh, you know. Like at someone's house. Maybe someone is playing a guitar. I just went to a Halloween party. People dressed up. But that's not important right now.

LYNX: Did you dress up?

BRIAN: No, I didn't. I thought about it. I had a costume. But then I felt like it was too much. So I didn't.

LYNX: That's a really sad story, Brian.

BRIAN: Is it? I guess it is. It's not really relevant.

LYNX: What was the costume?

BRIAN: Why are we talking about this? You know what? Let's go back to helping you get what you want so you can get out of here. Now, I should tell you the safe is on a timer so I can't open it right now.

LYNX: I'm just going to blast it and take it with me when I go.

BRIAN: Oh. Well, okay. I guess there's not much I can do to prevent that.

LYNX: What was your Halloween costume, Brian?

BRIAN: Oh, we don't need to—

LYNX: What was the costume? The one you didn't wear.

BRIAN: We're getting off track. What are your demands?

LYNX: First I need to know about your costume.

BRIAN: No. It's silly.

LYNX: Go on.

BRIAN: Oh. Well, Yeah. No. Okay. Well, I was going as Lily Mae.

LYNX: Oh.

BRIAN: Do you know, Lily Mae from the Jimmy's commercials?

LYNX: Yes, I know who that is.

BRIAN: And Louise who used to work here was going to be Jimmy. We were going together. But then she stopped working here.

LYNX: How did that happen?

BRIAN: I probably shouldn't say. For reasons of confidentiality.

LYNX: You sexually assaulted her?

BRIAN: No! No! Nothing like— She—uh— She was caught stealing.

JANE: Really?

BRIAN: Yes. And I had to let her go.

ANGIE: Is that why she broke up with you?

BRIAN: It was probably a contributing factor, yes.

LYNX: This costume thing just gets sadder and sadder.

BRIAN: I know.

LYNX: Go put it on.

BRIAN: What?

LYNX: I want to see your Lily Mae costume.

BRIAN: Oh, but—

LYNX: It's not here?

JANE: It's totally here. In his office.

BRIAN: I don't really think now's the time.

LYNX: It's the perfect time. Unless we should start hurting customers instead.

BRIAN: Don't hurt the customers.

LYNX: And staff.

BRIAN: That's not very nice.

LYNX: Go put it on. We'll wait.

BRIAN: But—

LYNX: And leave the office door open too so I don't have to bust it down to get to the safe.

BRIAN: Oh, but—

LYNX: This is the start of our negotiation, Brian. Are you going to put the costume on or are you going to make me angry?

BRIAN: I will put it on. On one condition.

LYNX: Oh, you got conditions.

BRIAN: You won't hurt anybody. While I'm gone. Okay?

LYNX: *(Thinks)* Okay.

(BRIAN exits. Everyone looks at LYNX and RAZOR. LYNX and RAZOR look at everyone.)

MEL: You're the one who's been blowing up Jimmy's franchises?

LYNX: Maybe.

JANE: *(Matter of fact)* We're all going to die.

(SUE JEAN whimpers.)

ANGIE: *(To her co-workers)* No one's gotten hurt yet, right? Just the buildings exploded.

MEL: Yeah.

JANE: Except that all that happened after hours. This is different.

LYNX: It's a little different. I wasn't sure our methods were working. And when methods don't work, you have to try new things.

JANE: I hate new things.

(RAZOR is looking at ANGIE.)

RAZOR: Hi.

ANGIE: What?

RAZOR: Hi.

ANGIE: Hi.

(ANGIE and RAZOR stare at each other.)

ANGIE: Why are you looking at me like that? Why is he looking at me like that?

LYNX: Who, Razor? I guess he is looking at you, isn't he? Razor, why are you looking at her like that? Yeah. Yup. I know what this is. Let me put it this way. I've only seen this once before. That was a special situation. See that glint in his eye? Yeah, that's real rare. Razor's real particular, but—I think he likes you. Razor, is that accurate? You like the lady?

RAZOR: *(Still staring at* ANGIE.*)* Hi.

ANGIE: What am I supposed to do?

LYNX: What do you want to do?

ANGIE: Are you sure he's not mistaken?

LYNX: Razor likes what Razor likes. Don't worry. He's into consent.

ANGIE: Um. Okay.

*(*MARTYNA *enters with her gun. She is covered in blood. She whispers something to* LYNX. LYNX *nods.)*

SUE JEAN: Um! My husband! Is he—

LYNX: *(Sharp)* Why are you talking?!!

SUE JEAN: Sorry.

*(*MARTYNA *approaches* SUE JEAN. MARTYNA *licks blood from her knuckles as she looks* SUE JEAN *in the eyes.)*

MARTYNA: Hello little lamb.

(Then MARTYNA *fans out to cover the room.* BRIAN *reenters dressed as Lily Mae. This costume must include a wig.)*

LYNX: Wow. That's some costume.

BRIAN: It's embarrassing.

LYNX: Don't be embarrassed. I think it works for you.

BRIAN: Really it only works if someone dresses as Jimmy too.

LYNX: Do you have that costume?

BRIAN: No. She stole that too.

LYNX: Shame.

BRIAN: Can I take it off now?

LYNX: Are you suggesting getting naked?

BRIAN: No. Not unless. . . No.

LYNX: Shame. Turn around.

(BRIAN *does*.)

LYNX: Yeah. I mean, I wouldn't say you look like her. You know what we should do? Let's do one of the commercials.

BRIAN: Why would we do that?

LYNX: I'm sure you have them memorized, right?

BRIAN: Why do you think that?

LYNX: You're kind of a Jimmy head. I can tell. I've seen it before. I bet you are in the fan club. Are you?

BRIAN: I mean. Yeah. I guess I'm kind of a Lily Mae fan.

LYNX: Sure. Who isn't?

BRIAN: It's what she represents.

LYNX: Right. What does she represent?

BRIAN: I don't know. Innocence? Wholesomeness? America?

LYNX: Wholesome, huh? Do you feel wholesome in that costume?

BRIAN: Not really.

LYNX: The food, is it wholesome?

BRIAN: Yes? I don't know. There are a lot of calories. It's filling.

LYNX: You think a chain restaurant run by a corporation can be wholesome?

BRIAN: I don't know.

LYNX: Well. People don't think. They feel. So. How do you feel about the corporation?

BRIAN: I don't know. What do you mean?

LYNX: You're right. Let's just do a commercial together. It's bonding, right? Building trust.

BRIAN: Um.

LYNX: Okay, so I'll be Jimmy. And you can be Lily Mae, okay. Oh! Let's get the wagon!

(Someone takes the wagon down and brings it over.)

LYNX: This is it, isn't it? It's the real wagon.

BRIAN: Yeah.

LYNX: All right. Get in it. Let's do one of the commercials.

(BRIAN sits on the wagon.)

LYNX: Which one…which one? Do you know the musical one?

BRIAN: Of course.

LYNX: Let's do that one. You ready?

BRIAN: Okay.

(Maybe the frame used earlier goes up for the commercial. LYNX plays Jimmy, BRIAN plays Lily Mae. They sing.)

LYNX: It's a beautful day.

BRIAN: I'm hungry.

LYNX: Do you see the trees sway?

BRIAN: But I'm hungry.

LYNX: Can you feel the sun's rays?

BRIAN: I'm hungry.

LYNX: Look up there, a Blue Jay.

BRIAN: I'm hungry!!!!

LYNX: Hey, Lily Mae,
What would you say
If we go
To a Jimmy's and stay
It's the finest and best
And it's always on the way
Lily Mae

BRIAN: Yum. Steak.

LYNX: It's a beautiful day.

BRIAN: For steak!

BRIAN & LYNX: Jimmy's All American: The American food America wants

BRIAN: *(As Lily Mae still)* I love you, Daddy.

(A moment, then—)

LYNX: I mean, that was pretty good.

BRIAN: Yeah. Thanks, I mean.

LYNX: I like your Lily Mae.

BRIAN: I've been working on it.

LYNX: Why?

BRIAN: What?

LYNX: Why are you obsessed with commercials from almost twenty years ago?

BRIAN: I mean I guess. There's something about her, right?

LYNX: Is there?

BRIAN: You can see it. She was just a normal kid but she was more than that. She had charisma. And she was happy. She was always so happy in those commercials. I guess I wish I was as happy when I was a kid. And also probably she was my first crush. You know? I wanted to be her and have her amazing father and live her glamorous but down-to-earth life. But really? Maybe? I wanted to drink soda across from her and talk to her.

LYNX: Where is she now?

RED: Heroin overdose.

LYNX: I didn't know that.

RED: Yeah. That's what Wikipedia says.

SUE JEAN: Yeah. That's true.

BRIAN: We don't like to talk about that here.

LYNX: So maybe she wasn't so happy.

BRIAN: Or maybe she tried it once. Let's not talk about it. Anyway, it may not be true. She might be still alive somewhere.

MEL: No, Brian.

LYNX: Nostalgia's a bitch huh?

BRIAN: No. I like nostalgia.

LYNX: But it's all fake, right? A big corporation playing on your emotions. The commercials make you happy, right? But the food sometimes makes you sick.

BRIAN: No. I mean. We do well here. I eat the food.

LYNX: Every day?

BRIAN: No, but—you can't just eat it every day.

LYNX: Why not? Isn't it wholesome?

BRIAN: That's not fair.

LYNX: I'm picking on you.

BRIAN: No you're not. You're threatening me with violence and firepower.

LYNX: Touché. Let's go get that safe. Martyna, with me.

BRIAN: Oh. Okay. Me too, huh?

(MARTYNA, LYNX and BRIAN exit. RAZOR is by ANGIE. Suddenly SUE JEAN screams.)

SUE JEAN: AAAAAAAAAAAAAAAHHHHHHH!

(Everyone looks at SUE JEAN.)

SUE JEAN: Sorry. Sorry. This isn't how I thought this night was going to go.

(Everyone looks away. RAZOR with ANGIE.)

RAZOR: Tell me about you.

ANGIE: Oh! Me? I don't know how much there is to tell. There is a hole inside me of course. But I don't drink to fill it. And I don't buy too many shoes. And I don't eat too much chocolate. I haven't found my compulsion yet I guess. So my emptiness just sits there waiting. And I don't know. I guess right now, I'm just trying to get through the day. Today is at least a bit different than yesterday.

RAZOR: Cause you're a hostage?

ANGIE: Yeah.

RAZOR: It's stressful.

ANGIE: Yeah, but, you know, it's different.

RAZOR: What do you do for fun?

ANGIE: Who has time for fun?

RAZOR: Yeah. Right.

ANGIE: I mean. I'm not against fun. I like fun. But at the end of the day I'm so tired. On my day off I sleep in. Might look at a magazine. Watch a show. Maybe cook something I want to eat.

RAZOR: I buy teacups.

ANGIE: You do?

RAZOR: I'm in a lot of teacup organizations. And we all have the ones we like best. From certain time periods or manufacturers. Or hand painted. Some prefer bone to porcelain. It's not really made out of bones though. That's just what it's called. I'm into the ornate ones. And I think about them a lot and I buy one finally after thinking about it a lot. And then I take a photo. Then I get a hammer and I smash the teacup. And I take another photo. That's what I like to do.

ANGIE: I think you should kiss me now.

(ANGIE *and* RAZOR *kiss. It gets passionate very quickly.* RED *and* JANE *watch.* RAZOR *and* ANGIE *head to a more private area.* JANE *and* RED *watch them go.*)

JANE: I just see them and I wonder why can't that be me.

RED: Yeah.

JANE: You know?

RED: Okay.

JANE: But it's not you. I mean it is you. You're not enough.

RED: Okay.

JANE: I want you to be more.

RED: More.

JANE: Yeah like more interesting. And more exciting. More attractive. Just more.

RED: Okay.

JANE: But you aren't. And you never will be.

RED: *(Unconcerned)* I know.

JANE: So.

RED: So you're done with me.

JANE: Yeah.

RED: Okay. Well I'm gonna get back to work. People still want their food.

JANE: This doesn't mean we're not going to have sex any more. I mean, if I know myself, we probably will, like at least a few more times.

RED: Yup. Okay. You know what I think? I think you don't really know what you want. I mean, what you think you want isn't really what you need.

JANE: You don't know what you're talking about.

RED: You don't know what you're talking about.

JANE: Um.

RED: YOU don't know what you're talking about.

JANE: Listen, Red. It's just over. That's all.

RED: I just want someone to sit on the couch next to me and watch a movie or some dumb show. Maybe we'll eat some Fritos. That's it. Listen to a song. Hold my hand. And I want it to be you. But if it's not you, it could be someone else. I'll wait. I'm patient. I don't know if I'm a catch or not but this stuff always works out for me. If it's not you, someone else will come along and sit on my couch with me. A customer or a waitress or someone I meet on the way to my car. That's just how it is.

JANE: I'm not replaceable.

RED: Okay.

JANE: You can't do that.

RED: Whatever. You need to hurt someone right now. You think it should be me. Do what you want. I like you. But I'm not nothing and you should know that.

JANE: I want to punch you.

RED: I know.

JANE: You're not indestructible.

RED: Hit me in the stomach. Not in the face.

(JANE *punches* RED *in the stomach a few times.*)

RED: You done?

(JANE *punches* RED *one more time.*)

JANE: Okay.

RED: I'll see you later.

JANE: I'll see you later.

(RED *exits to the kitchen.* MARTYNA *enters with* MARTY, *remember* MARTY? *He's bloody, gagged, tied to a chair on wheels. He has dynamite or plastic explosives all over him, maybe a timer too. It should look scary.* MARTYNA *wheels him out and deposits him at his table.* SUE JEAN *is there.*)

SUE JEAN: Marty!! Are you okay? Blink once if you're okay. Marty!

MARTY: Mmmmngh.

SUE JEAN: Can I take his gag off?

MARTYNA: No!

SUE JEAN: *(To* MARTYNA*)* What did you do to him?

MARTYNA: I roughed him. Just a little.

SUE JEAN: You're an animal.

MARTYNA: Yes. You are very pretty.

SUE JEAN: What?

MARTYNA: Does he tell you this? I bet he doesn't tell you this. Ever.

SUE JEAN: He used to.

MARTYNA: Used to is for shit.

SUE JEAN: I guess.

MARTYNA: Why are you with this coward?

SUE JEAN: My husband? He's my husband.

MARTYNA: It is as they say "too bad."

SUE JEAN: No, it's not.

MARTYNA: You love him?

SUE JEAN: Sure.

MARTYNA: Have you ever had the female orgasm?

SUE JEAN: I'm going to pretend you didn't say that.

MARTYNA: I am expert at manipulating the woman for the female orgasm. It is my talent. I am like bear.

SUE JEAN: Bear?

MARTYNA: Sexy bear.

SUE JEAN: Okay.

MARTYNA: You want I show you?

SUE JEAN: That's okay.

MARTYNA: You are saying no?

SUE JEAN: My husband is right here.

MARTYNA: He does not satisfy you. I can tell.

SUE JEAN: That's not fair.

MARTYNA: No. Is not fair. Life not fair. Life without good sex very sad life. But we persist.

SUE JEAN: You're dangerous.

MARTYNA: Yes.

SUE JEAN: You make me uncomfortable.

MARTYNA: Yes.

SUE JEAN: Can you go somewhere else?

MARTYNA: I don't think so. I need to keep an eye on the explosives.

SUE JEAN: Oh.

MARTYNA: And on you. On you I want to keep an eye too.

SUE JEAN: Oh.

MARTYNA: But now I sing song. For you.

(MARTYNA *sings a song in Russian. I don't know what this is. A folk song or something. She sings it like a cabaret singer. Right to* SUE JEAN. *It is a sexy cabaret song, in Russian. That thing, you know? And there is maybe a lot of contact with* SUE JEAN *during the song. Or is it just eye contact? When it is over she sits back down. She looks at* SUE JEAN. SUE JEAN *looks away.)*

(*A loud bang. Maybe some smoke. They blew the safe out of the wall.* BRIAN *enters carrying the safe.* LYNX *leads him in.* BRIAN *puts it down.)*

BRIAN: So you do what with this?

LYNX: I'll crack the safe later.

BRIAN: Okay. I mean, I'm not sure there's that much money in there.

LYNX: How many deposits?

BRIAN: Maybe one in there.

LYNX: It's not nothing.

BRIAN: No. So. You have the safe. You'll go now?

LYNX: Not quite.

BRIAN: What else do you want?

LYNX: I want you to start taking things off the wall and making a pile here.

BRIAN: The antiques?

LYNX: Yeah. Take them all down.

BRIAN: Some of them are really on there.

LYNX: You'll figure it out.

BRIAN: Well, okay. What for?

LYNX: You'll see. I'll help.

BRIAN: This is part of your plan?

LYNX: Just do it.

(BRIAN, LYNX *and some of the others start taking down the various wall decorations.* JANE *and* MEL *talk.*)

MEL: Hey.

JANE: Hey.

MEL: So, how you holding up?

JANE: Okay, you know, all things considered. You?

MEL: Okay. This is pretty crazy.

JANE: Yeah.

MEL: I know on TV and in the movies, this kind of thing happens all the time. But not really.

JANE: We'll be okay.

MEL: I'm supposed to say that. I'm the older sister.

JANE: Just barely.

MEL: We'll be okay.

JANE: You think?

MEL: Yeah.

JANE: If we're not—

MEL: No.

JANE: I'm just saying, we could die and if we do—

MEL: Stop.

JANE: I love you. That's all.

MEL: I love you too.

(MARTYNA, MARTY, SUE JEAN)

MARTYNA: You do not love him.

SUE JEAN: Yes I do.

MARTYNA: You are used to him. Is not the same as love. Your old shirt with the holes in it, you do not love this shirt. You are just used to it. But a new shirt come along, no holes, keep you warm, protect you, you throw the old shirt away, yes.

SUE JEAN: I don't know what you're saying.

MARTYNA: You know.

SUE JEAN: Yeah.

MARTYNA: You have thought about the divorce?

SUE JEAN: No. No. Yeah. We went through a rough patch. Didn't we, Marty? But we're coming out of that now.

MARTYNA: So you are happier with him than without him?

SUE JEAN: Well, how could I know that?

MARTYNA: That is a no. Have you been with a woman before?

SUE JEAN: No. No. Yeah. Sort of. Once. Nobody knows.

MARTYNA: How was it, with the woman?

SUE JEAN: It was…it was…nice.

MARTYNA: Yes. So I don't know you but this is how I do things, I fall in love at first sight and I tell you. You in turn run off with me and you belong to me and I protect you, better than he could and life is, you know fun and sometimes exciting. Like a lot of foods you never ate before.

SUE JEAN: I eat a lot of the same things over and over.

MARTYNA: So this is my offer. You don't have to say yes, but I think you should.

SUE JEAN: But maybe this time I wouldn't like being with a woman.

MARTYNA: Yes so come to the back with me and I will show you my talents.

SUE JEAN: I thought you had to stay with the explosives.

MARTYNA: No, that was bullshit.

(SUE JEAN looks at MARTY, then MARTYNA. MARTYNA kisses SUE JEAN. Then leads her off into the office or somewhere else backstage. JANE watches them go, sighs. BRIAN and LYNX have amassed a pile of things from the walls and food items from the back room, etc.)

BRIAN: So what are we doing?

LYNX: I want to destroy everything.

BRIAN: What do you mean everything?

LYNX: Everything. Watch.

(She smashes a trumpet or something with her baseball bat.)

BRIAN: Okay.

LYNX: More! More! More!

(BRIAN and the waitstaff bring a series of things and she hits them with her bat. Food, things they take off the walls. Etc. It's like a Gallagher show. LYNX sings.)

LYNX: Antique is just a word
For old crap no one wants
Unique is just absurd
For walls of restaurants
All the time we wasted
Wishing for yesterday
We were always wasted
I'll show you a new way
We tear it down
We smash it up

We leave nothing behind
When we're done with our smashing
There'll be nothing left to find
Smash the past
Smash the past
Smash
Smash
Smash the past
Smash the past
Smash
Smash
Smash

(This goes on for a while and then she turns to BRIAN.*)*

LYNX: What about you? You want to hit something?

BRIAN: No, that's okay.

LYNX: It'll relax you.

BRIAN: Nah, I'm fine.

LYNX: You're not fine. You have a lot of anger.

BRIAN: No.

LYNX: I know you do. Hit it with the bat.

*(*BRIAN *takes the bat. He takes a practice swing.)*

LYNX: You played baseball?

BRIAN: Yeah. Softball.

LYNX: Go on. Hit it.

(He does. He loves it.)

BRIAN: This is amazing.

ALL: We tear it down
We smash it up
We leave nothing behind
When we're done with our smashing
There'll be nothing left to find
Smash the past

Smash the past
Smash
Smash
Smash the past
Smash the past
Smash
Smash
Smash

JANE: Hit it, Lily Mae, hit it!

(BRIAN *laughs. He's having a good time. Everyone's having a good time.*)

LYNX: I told you. Didn't I tell you?

(JANE *brings ketchups or butter packets.*)

JANE: I hate this butter! (*Or "Let's marry these ketchups."*)

ALL: Smash the past
Smash the past
Smash
Smash
Smash the past
Smash the past

(RED *brings a beefsteak.*)

RED: Beat the shit out of this beefsteak.

(BRIAN *does. The feeling of a team coming together to destroy the place they work.*)

ALL: Smash the past
Smash the past
Smash
Smash
Smash the past
Smash the past

(*Then the wagon appears on the hitting block.*)

LYNX: STOP!! Not the wagon.

(The infectious joy goes out of the room.)

BRIAN: Why not the wagon? I hate that wagon. I hate that wagon so much!

LYNX: Not the wagon!!!!

*(*RAZOR *and* ANGIE *enter holding hands.)*

RAZOR: Everything okay?

LYNX: Fine. Fine. I just need the wagon. To take the safe out. Nobody do nothing. I have to—none of your business!

*(*LYNX *exits upset. To the bathroom maybe. Maybe she takes the wagon with her?* RAZOR *has the room covered.* MARTYNA *and* SUE JEAN *come back onstage. They look guilty, maybe a bit glowing. They sit again.* MARTY *looks at her.)*

SUE JEAN: Don't look at me like that, Marty. I know you know I know about you and Sandy. Yeah. That's right. So don't give me no stink eye.

MARTYNA: So I was telling the truth…about my talents, yes?

SUE JEAN: Yes.

MARTYNA: Good. So. I like you too. You will come with me?

SUE JEAN: It's tempting.

MARTYNA: Yes.

SUE JEAN: Let me think about it.

MARTYNA: Okay.

SUE JEAN: Okay?

MARTYNA: Okay. I will give you a few minutes. *(She walks away.)*

SUE JEAN: *(Sings)* Marty!
What can I say?

MARTY: *(Sings)* Mmph!

SUE JEAN: You did me wrong

MARTY: I guess not every day. *(Sings)*
Mmph!

SUE JEAN: I get to have something

MARTY: Marty *(Sings)*
Mmph!

SUE JEAN: I get to have my own way
It's not that I'm sick of you
Or tired of our life
It's not that I'm mad at you
It's not marital strife

MARTY: *(Sings)* Mmph!

SUE JEAN: I guess it's just something I had to do
Someone I had to be
I don't know what I'm doing
Mmph!
But I feel a little more like me.

MARTY: *(Sings like an impossible to understand solo here.)*
Mmph! Mppph! Mmmememekmmppphs!
Mmmphekfjjfjd! Meephfrr! Mppfee!

SUE JEAN: I'm not sorry
Marty
I'm not upset
Things have changed
Marty
Long since we met
It's untenable
Marty
But I have no regrets

MARTY: *(Sings)* Mmph!

SUE JEAN: It was love
Marty
It wasn't just sex.

MARTY: Mmmpf.

(RAZOR *and* ANGIE)

ANGIE: So that was…

RAZOR: Yes.

ANGIE: You do this a lot?

RAZOR: No.

ANGIE: Now what?

RAZOR: Whatever you want.

ANGIE: I want a mansion and lots of money and never have to work again.

RAZOR: Maybe not that.

ANGIE: Right.

RAZOR: But between you and me. Whatever you want.

(RED *comes out of the kitchen. He approaches* JANE.)

RED: Hey, so. There's still a hole in the floor of the kitchen. We could go out that way. Everyone from the kitchen already left.

JANE: Okay. But how do we leave without them noticing.

RED: I don't know. One at a time. I'll go check it out. See where the tunnel goes.

(RED *exits to the kitchen.* JANE *is about to tell* BRIAN *what* RED *said when* LYNX *returns. Was she crying? She wipes her face.)*

BRIAN: Are you okay?

LYNX: I don't know what you mean.

BRIAN: Okay. Um. What's your plan here? How can I get you and your guns out of my restaurant.

LYNX: Your restaurant?

BRIAN: I mean I don't own it.

LYNX: I thought we were past that, you and me. I thought you were starting to see things my way. I thought releasing all that anger in you would shake something loose.

BRIAN: Well, yeah. Maybe it did. Maybe…I don't know what. I might be confused.

LYNX: It's okay to be confused. This job is a terrible job.

BRIAN: No, it's—yeah I mean I wish there was more time off and I wish I wasn't so broke all the time still and I wish I didn't always think about productivity so much. And how can I ever retire and what if I get sick? I'm just trying to not have a heart attack before my fortieth birthday.

LYNX: Right. Well you're eager I'm sure to get back to that life.

BRIAN: I don't mean to complain. Times are rough right now for everybody.

LYNX: Not for Jimmy.

BRIAN: Well, probably not for him but he built this empire from nothing. He's a special case.

LYNX: Yeah.

BRIAN: I'm not special so…

LYNX: Well, I didn't say that.

BRIAN: I'm sorry I was complaining. I should be happy with what I have.

LYNX: Yeah, uh, I didn't mean that either.

BRIAN: Right. I guess someone like you can't understand settling for a lesser life. You're brave.

LYNX: I am.

BRIAN: I mean, I don't know what kind of person does what you do. You're insane probably but also brave. Aren't you?

LYNX: Okay. Well. Don't worry. We'll leave when we have what we want.

BRIAN: What do you want?

LYNX: Jimmy.

BRIAN: What?

LYNX: Yeah.

BRIAN: I don't think that's going to work.

LYNX: You don't think he'll sacrifice himself for his employees?

ANGIE: I don't think so.

LYNX: In any case, he's coming.

MEL: Jimmy's coming?

LYNX: I want to see his face when I blow the place up.

BRIAN: You wouldn't blow us all up, would you?

LYNX: Not if my demands are met.

BRIAN: What are your demands?

LYNX: I'll give him my demands when he comes.

MEL: Did you call him or something?

LYNX: I sent a letter. Like when you cut out the different letters from different magazines and paste it on a piece of paper? I did that.

BRIAN: Oh.

MEL: So then, he's coming for sure?

JANE: What if he doesn't come?

LYNX: He'll come. This time, he'll come.

BRIAN: I met him once. On the day I became manager here. I was here early, way earlier than anyone would have to be here. I guess I was eager to start. When I pulled in the parking lot, I saw a figure huddled by the front door. I was about to say to him, "We're not open yet", but then I saw who it was. He smiled. It was like a light turned on in my head. And he said, "Good luck, kid", and slipped something into my hand. It was the key to the back room on a Jimmy's logo keychain. And someone had written Brian on the back in permanent marker. Maybe he even wrote it in his own hand. When I looked up, he was gone. He didn't get into a car, he was just gone.

ANGIE: Wow.

BRIAN: They say he's touring his restaurants right now.

JANE: But where does he live normally?

BRIAN: Nashville.

MEL: Paris.

ANGIE: Saint Louis.

SUE JEAN: Miami.

BRIAN: He lives nowhere and everywhere. He is a vision and a myth.

LYNX: He's got a few houses. Mostly he lives in Chicago.

BRIAN: Chicago.

MEL, JANE, ANGIE: Chicago.

ANGIE: He met his second wife when she was a waitress at a Jimmy's in Ohio.

BRIAN: Oh yeah, I heard that.

SUE JEAN: Were all his wives waitresses? Is he married now?

ANGIE: I used to fantasize about him coming in one day and seeing me and taking me away from all this. But then that never happened. Life marched on. But now… *(She smiles at* RAZOR.*)*

*(*RAZOR *smiles back.* RED *enters, covered in dirt. He whispers to* JANE.*)*

JANE: Collapsed?

RED: *(Quiet)* Yeah. So, that won't work. Should I call the cops? I guess I should have done that a while ago. There's a phone in the kitchen and everything.

JANE: Don't do that. Jimmy's coming. I kind of want to meet him.

(Back to BRIAN*)*

BRIAN: I guess he dates a lot of the women from his restaurants.

JANE: Really?

ANGIE: Yeah. A lot.

BRIAN: I've heard stories. When all the managers get together. It happened at location thirty four. And ten. And eleven. And eighty two. And seventy five. And Wendy over in Springfield.

ANGIE: Wendy?! Really?

BRIAN: Yeah. It didn't last long. And thirty two. Mostly they run off with him and you never see them again and then months later you hear about him taking up with someone in Duluth.

RED: Some guys…are like that. *(He exits into the kitchen.)*

LYNX: That guy's the cook, right? How about some food while we wait for Jimmy? I'm hungry.

RED: *(Off)* All right. All right.

LYNX: Wash your hands. Is he always that dirty?

BRIAN: What did you just say?

LYNX: Me?

BRIAN: Say that again.

LYNX: What?

BRIAN: "I'm hungry."

LYNX: No.

BRIAN: Say it. Say it.

LYNX: No.

BRIAN: She's hungry.

JANE: So what?

BRIAN: Wow. Whoa. Can't you see? It's her. Lily Mae. *(He takes off his wig, throws it on the table.)*

MEL: No, it's not.

ANGIE: Lily Mae's dead.

BRIAN: Is she?

JANE: Isn't she?

MEL: It's not her.

BRIAN: It is. You are. I've watched those commercials over and over. I know how she says "I'm hungry." It's you. I know it is.

LYNX: Okay. Yeah. That's me. So what?

BRIAN: So what? SO WHAT? So all this time I was like for no reason someone is blowing up Jimmy Joints and then you turn out to be Lily Mae?

LYNX: I don't go by that name anymore.

BRIAN: What do you need the money from the safe for? What do you need anything for? You're richer than anybody.

LYNX: No, I'm not. Jimmy might be. Not me.

ANGIE: Jimmy's really your father?

LYNX: He was maybe my father of sorts for a few years. I was really useful to him when we were doing the commercials.

BRIAN: They still show them. The commercials.

LYNX: Yeah.

BRIAN: I mean I think the love between you in the commercials, you can feel it, coming through the screen. It's real. It's why people love Jimmy's.

LYNX: Things change. On the day he opened this place, he carried me in on his shoulders. He told me:

(LYNX *sings as lights change.*)

LYNX: I do it all for you
My darling
I know we will be huge
My love
Rich fancy and famous
My dear
I owe it all to you
He took my toys away
And hung them on the wall
We made a million commercials
And I was in them all
Then a waitresss or two
Then Daddy didn't come home
He left my mom and me
He left us all alone
And then it was my birthday
Daddy didn't call
Then we were evicted
Daddy didn't call
Evicted five more times
Daddy didn't call

Graduated high school
Daddy didn't call
Had my first heart broken
Daddy didn't call
Then the day mama died
Heart stopped at fifty-five
The drugs didn't help
I couldn't help
But I tried
And Daddy never called.
I do it all for you
My darling
I know we will be huge
My love
Rich fancy and famous
My dear
I owe it all to you
But Daddy never called
Never called
Never called
Never called
Never called
Never called
Never called
Never called
Never called

BRIAN: Oh. I thought. I guess I always assumed it was amazing to be Lily Mae.

LYNX: He hasn't really been part of my life since I was seven.

BRIAN: So you're blowing up his restaurants? Why don't you just call him?

LYNX: (Shouted, not sung) WHY DOESN'T HE CALL ME? HUH? WHY DOESN'T HE CALL ME?

(LYNX stalks off to the kitchen.)

(A beat. With ANGIE *and* RAZOR*)*

ANGIE: You think you might be mistaken? About me. And your feelings. About me.

RAZOR: I'm not mistaken. Sometimes you just know.

ANGIE: But what if it doesn't last?

RAZOR: How long do you want it to last?

ANGIE: I don't know. Is it going to be over at the end of the day?

RAZOR: Not for me.

ANGIE: Until we die of old age?

RAZOR: Maybe.

ANGIE: Maybe you'll get glasses or something or get hit on the head and then you'll see me. Or there will be a moment when I'm selfish or a coward and you'll hate me for it.

RAZOR: I'm not worried about it.

ANGIE: You know what happened last time? He just left. No note. No nothing. I come back from work and all his stuff is gone. His phone is disconnected. Who knows where he went. Probably shacking up with someone else.

RAZOR: No one should treat you that way. If you want, I can find him. That's something I can do. And I could make him suffer if that's what you want or apologize or you know make it harder to be him every day. You want me to do that?

ANGIE: You'd do that?

RAZOR: If you want.

ANGIE: No, no. That's okay. You don't have to do that.

RAZOR: Think about it.

ANGIE: Maybe. No. Maybe.

(MEL *approaches a stunned* BRIAN.)

MEL: You okay?

BRIAN: I can't believe I finally met Lily Mae and she's threatening to kill me.

MEL: Life can be funny I guess.

BRIAN: I thought I understood things about how the world works. How good people are rewarded for working hard. Or something. I don't know. People are good, aren't they? I mean deep down.

MEL: I think so.

BRIAN: I don't know.

MEL: At least she didn't shoot you. Or me. Or anyone. Yet.

BRIAN: I didn't mean her.

MEL: Oh.

(LYNX *enters eating some steak or something.*)

JANE: How is it?

LYNX: It's good. It tastes better than it's supposed to taste.

JANE: Red kind of puts his own spin on it.

LYNX: Huh.

(*Enter* WILLIAM, *after taking the chains off the doors. He is holding an ipad or clipboard or whatever. Talks into a headset or bluetooth*)

WILLIAM: Yes, well, yes. Okay. Bye.

LYNX: Where is he?

WILLIAM: He sent me.

LYNX: No. No. No. NO!

ANGIE: Who is this?

BRIAN: It's Jimmy's personal assistant.

JANE, MEL, RED: William.

RED: William, cool.

SUE JEAN: Really? That's William?

WILLIAM: What happened here?

BRIAN: There was, um, some smashing.

WILLIAM: I see.

LYNX: I want to talk to him.

WILLIAM: He doesn't want to talk to you. He said, "I don't negotiate with terrorists".

LYNX: I'm not. That's not. William, you know that's not what this is.

WILLIAM: You did set fires in two of his locations.

LYNX: They were explosions.

WILLIAM: Thankfully insurance will cover it. In fact, we might come out ahead when all is said and done. In any case, he wants me to say you should leave and if you don't leave the SWAT team will come and take you away.

LYNX: What SWAT team?

WILLIAM: I didn't call them. Not yet.

LYNX: He's really not coming?

WILLIAM: He's really not.

LYNX: But I'm here. Where it all started. I was here the first day it opened. He took all my toys away and hung them up.

WILLIAM: I know.

LYNX: I thought he would come. That's really disappointing. When I get disappointed, I get violent. Should I get violent, William? What if I blew this place up?

ANGIE: Excuse me. I'm sorry, but could you not-- Can you not blow this place up? I need this job. My car broke down last month and I'm broke now so if I don't work next week, I'll be evicted.

WILLIAM: Yeah, don't blow anything up. It's…a lot of paperwork. Oh, Mel's here. Hi Mel.

MEL: Hi.

WILLIAM: So you two have met then.

LYNX: What?

WILLIAM: Your father's girlfriend.

MEL: Fiancée.

WILLIAM: Fiancée.

LYNX: Her? Seriously?

JANE: Why didn't you say anything?

LYNX: Seriously?

MEL: I didn't know how to bring it up. I was waiting for the right moment.

LYNX: Seriously?!!

ANGIE: You should have told us.

JANE: You should have told me.

BRIAN: Where did you meet him?

MEL: In the parking lot.

BRIAN: Sure. That makes sense.

LYNX: I want to talk to him. I'm not leaving until I talk to him.

(WILLIAM *sighs.*)

WILLIAM: He doesn't want to talk to you.

LYNX: Do I need to threaten you with bodily harm, William?

WILLIAM: Come on, Lilypie.

LYNX: Don't call me that.

WILLIAM: All right. Let me see if I can get him. *(He makes a call.)* She says she won't leave until she talks to you. I know. Yes. Well. I agree. I could bring in the SWAT team. I don't know if… Right but I don't know if…yes. Yes. Of course. No. *(To* LYNX*)* Here.

LYNX: Hello. Why do you think? That's hardly… Did you read the letter? Because— You need to come down here right now… Because William is never far from where you are. Stop talking. Stop TALKING! You're not talking your way out of this. Get down here right now. No because if you send the SWAT team I'll talk to the press. How would they like to hear about Lily Mae in an armed standoff at a Jimmy's? Good because if I have to wait for more than five minutes, I'm cutting off pieces of William one at a time. And when you're done with him I start in on your new girlfriend. Oh yeah? Try me!

*(*MEL *has been standing there. She reaches for the phone.* LYNX *doesn't give it to her.)*

LYNX: He hung up.

MEL: Oh. I thought he might want to talk to me.

*(*WILLIAM *takes the phone back.)*

WILLIAM: You aren't really going to—

MEL: She wouldn't—

LYNX: Not if he gets here soon.

MARTYNA: *(Approaches with a large knife drawn.)* I like to start with ears. More fun than fingers.

LYNX: Not yet.

MARTYNA: Clock is ticking.

*(*WILLIAM *wilts. Texts a furious text)*

BRIAN: Can I talk to you?

(LYNX *goes with* BRIAN *off to the side.*)

BRIAN: I want to say— *(Sings)*
Lily Mae
You've put me in a pickle
You've left me high and dry
A drop becomes a trickle
When rain falls from the sky
I mean my heart is fickle
And the water's getting high
Lily Mae

LYNX: Um.

BRIAN: Let me finish.
You're the thing I was never looking for to find the
   thing I want.
You're the reason I started working in this stupid
   restaurant.

LYNX: Um.

BRIAN: Reason went out the window when I saw you
   standing there
Not just your eyes, shape of your face or color of your
   hair
It's the Lily Mae about you that Lily Mae's my heart
It Lily made me feel this way, and Lily might make me
   start
The rumble in my brambles
The buzz around my brain
Lily Mae you've Lily made
Me completely insane
I don't know where I'm going
But I know I'll follow you
Anything you want or wish
I'll help it all come true
And if that means I have to die—

(LYNX *stops* BRIAN *with a kiss. The music stops.*)

LYNX: Let's talk about this later. Things change in the moment. You might not feel that way in five minutes.

BRIAN: No, but—

LYNX: Let's talk about it after.

BRIAN: But—

LYNX: After!

MARTYNA: He's not coming.

(MARTYNA *grazes* WILLIAM'*s ear with her knife, about to cut.*)

WILLIAM: He'll be here! He'll be here! Give me one more minute!

(*Enter* JIMMY.)

JIMMY: What's going on here?

(*Everybody stares. No one says anything.*)

SUE JEAN: It's Jimmy!

JIMMY: What are you doing to my restaurants?

LYNX: Remodeling.

JIMMY: That's cute. That's real cute. Let's get this place back up and running. Let's clean up this mess. Let me talk to this young lady and you all can get back to your business. Who's in charge here?

BRIAN: I—

(*Everybody starts trying to look busy.*)

LYNX: Stop! I think they should all hear this.

JIMMY: Hear what? There's nothing to hear. You're angry at me and you're going to punish all these nice folks because of it.

LYNX: You don't think I should be mad at you?

JIMMY: Honestly, you're better off without me. I was not good at parenthood. I couldn't do it. Not really. Not everyone can. I tried to pretend for a while but I just couldn't. Your mother didn't want me around anyway so it was for the best.

LYNX: That's…infuriating.

JIMMY: Okay so can they get back to work now?

LYNX: Maybe you couldn't take care of me, but you can still take care of them.

JIMMY: Hi, Sweetie.

MEL: Hi, Honey.

LYNX: You don't pay them well.

(*Everyone stops and looks at* JIMMY.)

JIMMY: Industrywide I think we're competitive.

LYNX: So you pay them shit like everyone else does.

JIMMY: It's a family here. Times are tough but we do what we can for everyone.

LYNX: Is that true?

JANE: I mean it would be nice to get insurance.

BRIAN: And paid sick days.

ANGIE: And a raise.

RED: And more flexibility with the menu. Why can't I make my lobster thermidor? And what's wrong with a white wine glaze, anyway? And what do you have against radishes? Or chocolate molten lava cake?

BRIAN: That might be a little off topic.

RED: Or a Cornish hen. The problem with this place is the lack of appreciation for Cornish hen.

JIMMY: Um. I'm going to take all of this into consideration. William, are you taking notes?

WILLIAM: Yes, sir.

JIMMY: Great! I can bring up all these things to the board. You just have to speak up. How would I know about how strongly you feel about the Corned hen?

RED: Cornish.

LYNX: No. The time for pretending to consider things is over. Wipe that smile off your face. You can't glad-hand your way through this. You left me behind. And you left them behind too. And now you'll pay.

JIMMY: That's hurtful. I think of you all the time. I always wonder about you. I ask William to keep up with what you're doing?

LYNX: William, you spy on me for my dad?

WILLIAM: Uh, I uh—

LYNX: It's too late. For me and you.

JIMMY: Don't say that.

LYNX: But it's not too late to make it up to them.

JIMMY: I'm not going to be held hostage by you.

LYNX: I'm just asking you to do the right thing for once. You posted record profits every quarter for the last two years.

JIMMY: Right. We're doing really well.

LYNX: But they're all living paycheck to paycheck. *(Silence)* You understand what I'm saying? Tell me you understand what I'm saying.

JIMMY: We can have this conversation over lunch if you want. Like civilized people. But I won't have this conversation with a gun to my head.

LYNX: I feel like you're still not taking me seriously.

(She shoots him in the leg.)

JIMMY: Ah! What the? Ahh.

(WILLIAM *runs to him starts applying pressure to the wound.* MEL *runs over with ice.*)

MEL: What is wrong with you?!

WILLIAM: Call an ambulance!

LYNX: Not yet. Not until you agree to my demands.

JIMMY: You shot me!

LYNX: The next one goes into your head.

WILLIAM: He'll bleed out.

LYNX: Then he should agree to my demands.

JIMMY: What are your demands?

LYNX: I want a ten dollar an hour increase for all employees immediately. Is that enough?

BRIAN: Uh, yeah.

LYNX: And yearly cost of living increases of at least a dollar an hour.

JIMMY: Sweetie.

LYNX: Don't sweetie me. Every employee working more than twenty hours gets insurance. And paid sick leave. And paternity leave. And vacation days.

JIMMY: Uh. That's a lot of money. I need to talk to—

LYNX: And then after you've done that, you step down and announce that I'm taking over control of the company.

JIMMY: But—

LYNX: You'll do this. All this. Or else.

JIMMY: Or else—

LYNX: I let you die right here right now.

MEL: No.

JIMMY: Lily Mae, be reasonable.

LYNX: I am reasonable. I understand you're just doing what everyone else is doing. But it's rotten and Jimmy's Restaurant used to mean something. Something good. Don't you want it to mean something good again?

WILLIAM: He doesn't look so good. We need to get you to the hospital.

JIMMY: Okay. Okay.

(LYNX gives JIMMY a contract to sign.)

JIMMY: I don't have time to read all this.

LYNX: Just sign it.

(JIMMY signs it.)

LYNX: Get him out of here.

(WILLIAM and MEL and maybe someone else start to carry him out.)

LYNX: Wait! Daddy? I-- nevermind. No, I need to know. Why don't you love me?

JIMMY: There are different kinds of love.

LYNX: No. There is love and there is not love. Fucker.

(They continue to drag JIMMY out.)

JANE: Are you leaving? Now?

MEL: It's probably best.

(WILLIAM, JIMMY, MEL exit.)

MEL: *(To JANE)* I'll…I'll call you.

(JANE nods. Everyone watches them go.)

LYNX: That was—I'm going to go to your office.

BRIAN: You want company?

(LYNX nods. Exit BRIAN and LYNX.)

(MARTYNA and SUE JEAN and MARTY.)

MARTYNA: So you leave with me, yes. And we have adventures and live exciting life sometimes. Other times just normal lesbian American life.

SUE JEAN: Let me just talk to Marty.

MARTYNA: Okay.

(MARTYNA *takes off gag and everything. She walks out of earshot.*)

MARTY: Water.

(SUE JEAN *gives him water, maybe taking from another table.* MARTY *drinks.*)

MARTY: The Eastern European, huh?

SUE JEAN: Yeah.

MARTY: Huh.

SUE JEAN: I'm sorry.

MARTY: Okay.

SUE JEAN: I'll come back for my stuff.

MARTY: Okay.

SUE JEAN: Or maybe I won't.

MARTY: Okay.

SUE JEAN: Anyway, Happy Birthday.

MARTY: *(Taking it in stride)* Thanks. Thanks, Sue Jean. I admit I'm a bit disappointed.

SUE JEAN: Yeah.

MARTY: But I'm used to disappointment. I guess I got a story to tell.

SUE JEAN: Yeah.

MARTY: I won't forget this birthday.

SUE JEAN: I guess you won't.

MARTY: You take care of yourself, okay?

SUE JEAN: Okay.

MARTY: I guess I got to get a new phone.

(SUE JEAN *goes off with* MARTYNA *to pack or something. They exit.)*

(ANGIE *and* RAZOR)

ANGIE: Can you stay in one place?

RAZOR: I don't know. No. I don't. I can't.

ANGIE: I'm from here. I like it here. My friends are here. My family. I don't want to leave.

RAZOR: The things I could show you. Prague. Disney World. Tibet. The moon.

ANGIE: The moon?

RAZOR: Florida.

ANGIE: I don't need that.

RAZOR: I need you.

ANGIE: That's nice. But, no you don't. Or you would stay here. In my little apartment.

RAZOR: I can't. Not for long.

ANGIE: It was nice to meet you. It was nice to be special.

RAZOR: I could still break your ex's legs.

ANGIE: I'll think about it.

RAZOR: I could still call you.

ANGIE: Maybe. Okay. Call me. I'll be here.

(RED *enters, approaches* JANE.)

RED: Hey, kid.

JANE: Hey.

RED: What are you doing tonight?

JANE: I dunno.

RED: Want to come over and watch some TV?

JANE: Um. Okay. Just this once.

RED: Okay.

JANE: Just this once.

(BRIAN *and* LYNX *return. The safe is in the wagon and* LYNX *is pulling it.*)

BRIAN: *(To group)* Hey everyone! Can I get your attention? Hi. Sorry. Um. I'm going to go help Lynx, maybe work for corporate or just take some time off I don't know. Figure some stuff out. Angie, you want to be manager?

ANGIE: Oh! Yeah. Okay, yeah.

BRIAN: I'll let corporate know. They'll make it official.

ANGIE: Thanks!

BRIAN: You'll like it. Maybe. It's just like being a server but it's not like that at all.

ANGIE: Okay. It doesn't look too hard.

BRIAN: Yeah. Well.

ANGIE: Does that mean Jimmy will approach me in the parking lot? Because I pepper spray anyone who approaches me in the parking lot.

BRIAN: You do it your way. *(Tosses her keychain)* Good luck, kid.

ANGIE: I'm gonna miss you.

(ANGIE *hugs* BRIAN. *So does* JANE. RED *shakes his hand.*)

RED: Take care of yourself.

JANE: Bye, Brian.

LYNX: *(To* BRIAN*)* You coming?

BRIAN: Yeah. Where are we going?

LYNX: Somewhere else.

BRIAN: Okay.

(LYNX and BRIAN and the wagon go. MARTYNA and SUE JEAN and RAZOR follow.)

(JANE, ANGIE, RED, MARTY left on the stage. ANGIE begins to sing as they get back to work.)

ANGIE: Okay. Back to work, everybody.

(They might groan or respond in some way.)

ANGIE: Nothing bad can ever happen at Jimmy's
  Beefsteak Place
When you're here, you're comfy and you're home
Nothing bad can ever happen at Jimmy's Beefsteak
  Place
When you're here, you'll never be alone.

RED: Two steaks for the price of one steak

JANE: All you can eat filler uppers

RED: And steak.

JANE: Onions in all different size and shape

RED: And steak.

JANE: Deep fried potato dippers

RED: And steak.

MARTY: Chicken flavored dumplings

RED: And steak.

ANGIE: And the salad bar is all that you can take.
Nothing bad can ever happen at Jimmy's Beefsteak
  Place
When you're here, you're comfy and you're home
Nothing bad can ever happen at Jimmy's Beefsteak
  Place
When you're here, you'll never be alone.

ANGIE, RED, JANE, MARTY: Nothing bad can ever
  happen at Jimmy's Beefsteak Place

When you're here, you're comfy and you're home
Nothing bad can ever happen at Jimmy's Beefsteak
    Place
When you're here, you'll never be alone.

(The whole cast enters and sings. This becomes the curtain call.)

EVERYONE: Nothing bad can ever happen at Jimmy's
    Beefsteak Place
When you're here, you're comfy and you're home
Nothing bad can ever happen at Jimmy's Beefsteak
    Place
When you're here, you'll never be alone.

END OF PLAY

www.ingramcontent.com/pod-product-compliance
Lightning Source LLC
Chambersburg PA
CBHW052221090426
42741CB00010B/2633